How to Make People Feel Awkward at Work

(without getting reported to HR... probably)

Andrew Worden

Copyright © 2020 Andrew Worden

All rights reserved.

ISBN: 9798643387374

This quick start guide to making people feel awkward at work will give you 50 tips and tricks to help you master the craft of making any situation uncomfortable.

Everybody, and I mean everybody, is interested in being more awkward at work, but few people know how to pull it off. This book will help you achieve levels of awkwardness previously thought impossible!

CONTENTS

1	Awkwardness	1
2	More Awkwardness	8
3	More Awkwardness	13
4	More Awkwardness	19
5	More Awkwardness	24
6	More Awkwardness	27
7	More Awkwardness	35
8	More Awkwardness	42
9	More Awkwardness	56
10	More Awkwardness	63

(Jokes on you - I don't even think there's 63 pages in this book)

Turn the page for a special surprise!

Haha gotcha!

It's just a blank page.

Okay, let's get started:

How should you respond when a co-worker asks, "How was your weekend?"

You have 3 good options here:

1. "Well I'm still waiting for the cops to get back to me."
2. "I couldn't sleep at all because you-know-who's in town."
3. "Pretty good. The rash seems to be getting better."

Regardless of your response, it's important to walk away right after you respond without providing any follow up information.

Leave sticky note on other people's food in the fridge that reads "Let me know if you don't finish this."

Respond to all your emails with phone calls.

If anyone asks why you didn't just email them back, then tell them that you haven't spoken to them in a while and wanted to catch up (even if you've never spoken to them before).

Ring ring

"Hey, I'm just responding to your email."

Whenever someone is getting coffee make sure to say, "I put something special in there," laugh, and then say, "just kidding," while sipping your coffee and not breaking eye contact.

When talking with someone in a causal conversation don't make eye contact, just stare directly at their forehead the entire time.

Don't forget to stare with the hot intensity of a thousand suns.

Sing along under your breath to whatever song is playing in your headphones.

Remember, when you have your headphones on, that means no one else can hear you.

At least once a day, go up for a high five and then pull it away while shouting, "TOO SLOW!"

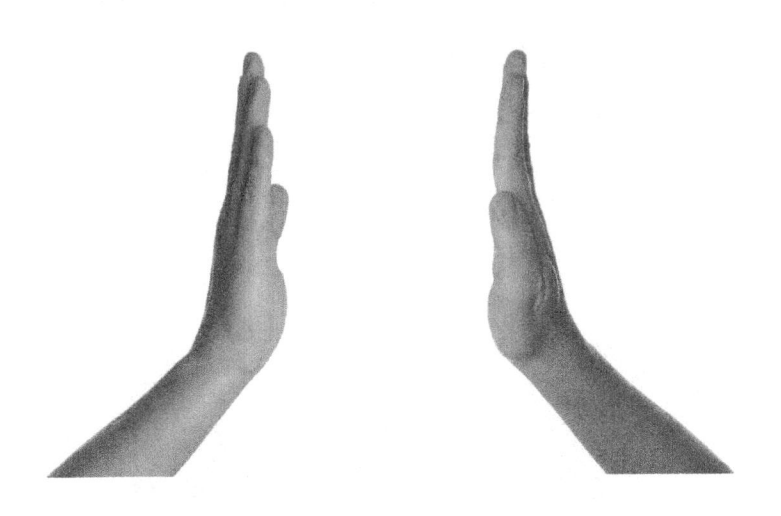

Double points if you take your hand and glide it through your hair after dodging your co-worker's failed attempt.

You're in a situation where the restroom is completely quiet. You and I both know that's unacceptable. Make your presence known by simply announcing, "Wow, that burrito last night was big mistake."

If you're a remote employee, make sure to tell people every single day that you're working from home.

The first few times will get some laughs.

The next few times will get some awkward chuckles.

After that it's just awkward.

There's literally never a wrong time for a dad joke.

Here's some good starters:

- Why couldn't the prospector buy alcohol? Because he was a miner!
- How does a bird deposit their checks? They go to the nearest branch.
- What kind of drink does a boxer serve at a party? Punch!
- How many apples did the math equation buy? Sum.
- Why do soccer players like spicy food? It's got a kick to it!
- What does a supportive tree say? "I'm rooting for you!"

Hold the door open for someone who's way too far away.

If two other people are having a private conversation, then you should take that as an open invitation.

Walk up and start talking about something else entirely.

If they don't immediately engage then it's always appropriate to speak a little louder.

If you haven't met your awkward quota for the day, an easy way to gain momentum is to accidentally drop something on the ground.

Bonus points for food or something breakable that you must clean up.

The longer you drag this out the more awkward the situation gets.

If you're mid-conversation and need to burp, then no worries. Just continue to talk while doing that sweet hiccup burp combo you've mastered over the years.

Personal bubbles were meant to be popped. It's important to stand awfully close to everyone you talk to.

Everybody loves a close-talker.

If someone tells you a joke, even if you find it hilarious, reply with a sad look and say, "What did you just say to me?"

Remembering people's names is optional.

On a regular basis you need to mispronounce or straight up butcher people's names.

"Hey Cheryl!"

"...It's Mark..."

If you're doing a PowerPoint presentation, add a GIF of a cat.

Bonus points if you're presenting to an executive.

If you make a tiny mistake, then it's important to bring up that mistake as many times as possible.

It's impossible to make a mountain without a molehill.

For example, forgetting your lunch and then telling everyone every hour how you can't believe you forgot your lunch.

If you need to talk to someone, use the opportunity to stand behind them silently for a few seconds before engaging in conversation.

During a meeting start rubbing your eye and looking up at the ceiling. Proceed to get on your hands and knees and start looking for your contacts on the floor.

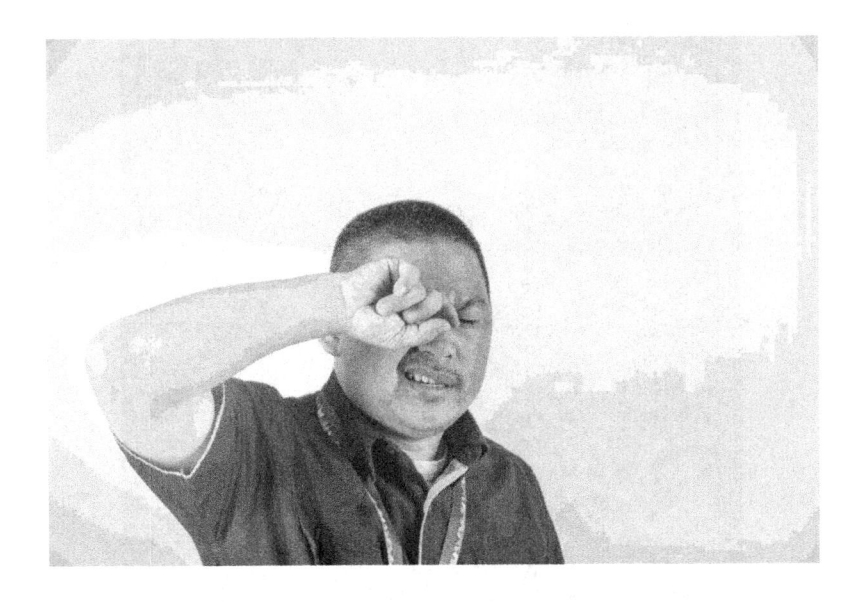

Hopefully, some people in the room realize that you don't wear contacts.

Periodically stop and say, "Eww, do you smell that?" and sniff the person next to you.

No matter what your current conversation is about, stop it and say something like, "It's really awkward right now" and let the silence speak for itself.

Walk around the office without any shoes on.

Extra credit if you have serious foot odor.

Put Christmas lights up around your desk during the middle of summer.

Make sure to take them down before the holiday season.

Get your co-worker's attention from across the room, hold up a blank piece of paper and point it, and then laugh as you sit back down.

Push a door that says pull.

The longer you try, the more awkward it gets.

Go up to someone, shake their hand, and as soon as the shake is over, smell your hand vigorously while staring at the victim.

If you use the male restroom and there's several urinals, it's your duty to always choose the urinal directly next to someone even if there are other ones available.

Try to make direct eye contact conversation if you're feeling particularly bold.

No matter how long the conversation is, you should never blink.

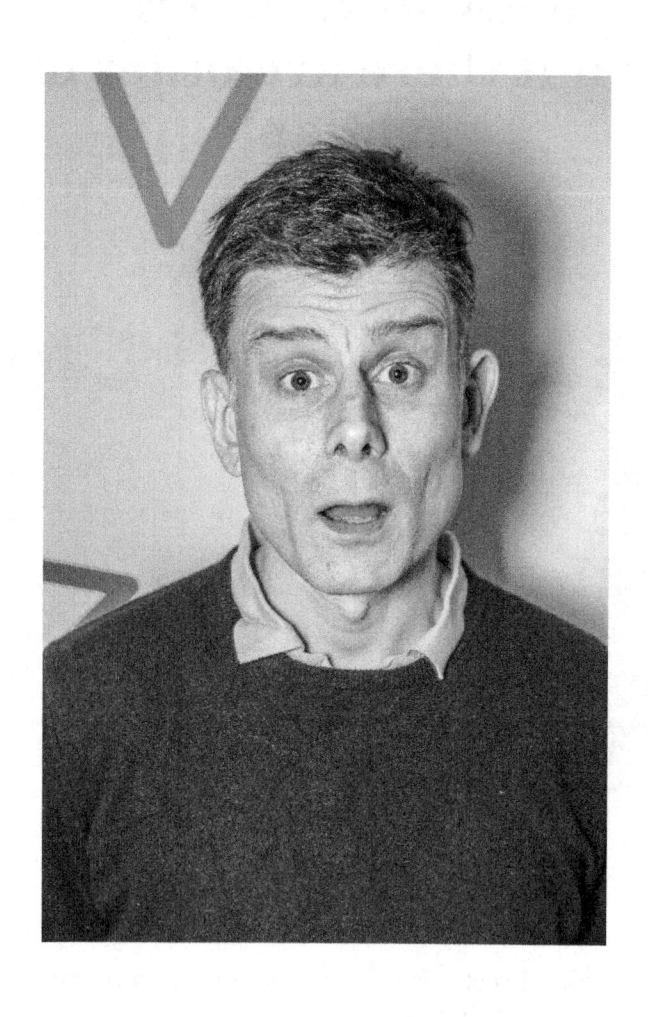

If someone starts doing their dishes, walk up and start washing your hands in the same sink.

Start a very personal phone call right next to someone's desk.

"No, it's fine... You can give me the test results."

Starts crying

It's a perfectly normal bodily function. Just fart.

Excuse yourself in the middle of meeting and come back in a completely different outfit.

If anyone asks why you changed your clothes, act like you have no idea what they're talking about.

If someone goes in for a fist bump, try to shake their hand.

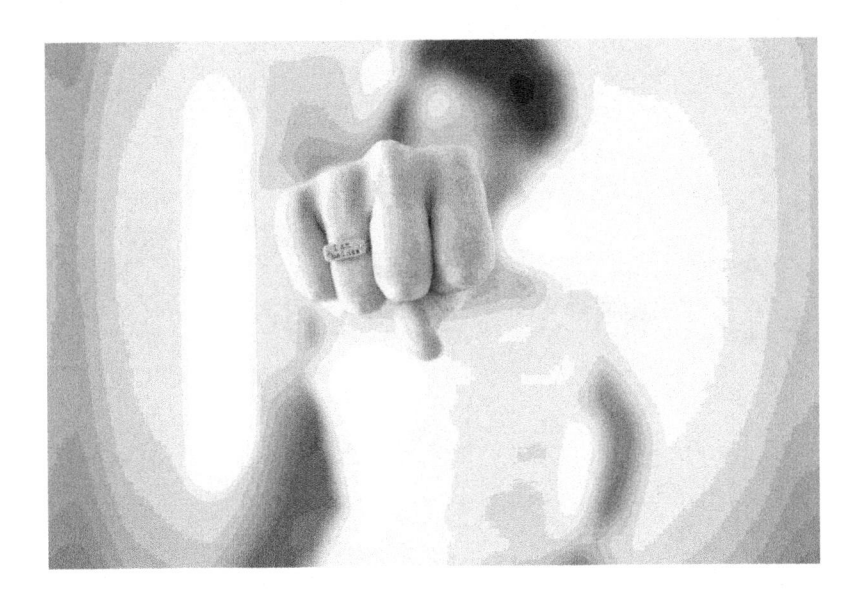

And if they try to shake your hand, go in for a fist bump.

Continue this process until they walk away.

Walk around the office and have everyone sign a birthday card for someone they don't know.

Say goodbye to a co-worker before they plan on leaving.

It becomes awkward once they realize you aren't leaving.

Even more awkward if the co-worker was leaving and they hadn't told anyone...

Every time you microwave something, say that you left aluminum foil on it and pretend to freak out.

"Oh noooo... Did I forget to take off the aluminum foil again?? Ahhh just kidding!"

"Had you goin' there for a second though, didn't I?"

Wave at someone you don't actually know.

Answer your phone while someone else is talking to you, even if it's not ringing.

Get up and use someone else's stapler every time you need to staple something.

Even if you have your own stapler at your desk.

You can use this same tactic for scissors and tape.

If you're walking back to your car and see a co-worker, pretend to get into their car, laugh, and say, "Oh sorry, I thought this was my car!"

Apparently, my buddy Matt does this all the time.

When someone is leaving work for the day, say, "Have a nice flight!"

Every time someone says hi to you, look confused and respond with what you're doing.

"Hi Andrew!"

"...I'm stapling papers..."

Google search a co-worker's name on your phone, start talking to them, and during the conversation pull out your phone to show them something and stumble around like you didn't want them to see it.

Borderline HR reportable...

If someone tells you a story, then wait 2 hours and tell them the same exact story as if it happened to you.

Laugh out loud every time you read something funny on your phone or computer. (Don't hold back)

It's perfectly fine to make a scene.

To the person I work with: You know who you are...

When approaching a co-worker walking the opposite direction in the hallway and you both do the uncomfortable bob and weave, but just end up getting in each other's way.

This is the perfect excuse to say, "That's the first dance I haven't paid for in weeks."

While in a quiet meeting, take a large gulp of water, have it go down the wrong pipe, and spastically cough for at least a minute.

Face the wrong way in an elevator full of people.

Wow! You made it to the end!

Now go out there and make the world a little more awkward!

You   Me

If you have enjoyed (most of) my material, then a review would be greatly appreciated!

If you're feeling generous you can go to www.amazon.com, search for "How to Make People Feel Awkward at Work", click this book in the search results, scroll down to the Reviews section, and click the "Write a customer review" button.

Thank you so much for reading. I hope you had a great time!

Made in the USA
Monee, IL
09 May 2020